Utterances and Incantations
Women, Poetry and Dub

Edited by
Afua Cooper

Sister Vision
Black Women and Women of Colour Press

99 00 01 02 SVP 4 3 2 1

Canadian Cataloguing in Publication Data
Main entry under title:
Utterances and incantations: women, poetry and dub
Includes bibliographical references
ISBN 0-896705-28-6

1. Canadian Poetry (English) – Women authors* 2. Canadian poetry
(English) – 20th century.* 3. Caribbean poetry (English) – Women
authors. 4. Caribbean poetry (English) – 20th century.
I. Cooper, Afua
PS8283.W6U87 1999   C811'5408'09287   C99–930914-5
PR9195.3.U87 1999

Cover Art: © Stephanie Martin
Book Design: Stephanie Martin
Editor for the Press: Makeda Silvera

Sister Vision Press gratefully acknowledges the financial support of
the Canada Council towards its publishing program.

The editor acknowledges the financial support of
the Ontario Arts Council.

Represented in Canada by the Literary Press Group
Distributed in Canada and the United States by
the University of Toronto Press
Represented in Britain by Turnaround Distribution

Printed in Canada by union labour

SISTER VISION
Black Women and Women of Colour Press
P.O. Box 217, Station E
Toronto, Ontario
Canada M6H 4E2
email: sisvis@web.net

*This book is dedicated to two Caribbean women
who fought to free the Word:
Queen Nanny of the Jamaica Portland Maroons
and the
Honourable Louise Bennett-Coverley (Miss Lou)*

Acknowledgements

To all the poets in this volume, for your support, love, and big heartedness. You put up wid my midnight calls, early morning visits, and plenty baddarashan. You are moon rays, nuff love. To Faybienne Miranda, matriarch of words, thanks for the reasoning and the level vibes. To the women of Sister Vision Press — Makeda Silvera and Stephanie Martin — for your four-eye sight. You are special. To Pamela Mordecai, for your insightful suggestions, and critical comments, (full of love). To Anilia Soyinka for your crucial feedback, respect. To Johnny Oboe, for the priority post and the quick e-mail responses, apprecilove. To Klive Walker, thanks for the music and poetry palavahs. To Madiou Diallo for chauffeuring me around to poets' homes, you are my Sulayman. To the dawtas, Lamarana and Habiba, whose patience and impatience pushed this book to completion, you are my light and my beloved. And to di great foremadda, Penda (Alison Parkinson) who sat on the banks of Roaring River and uttered, thanks for the inspiration. An dere mus be nuff more who mi nuh name, but who help to mek dis book possible. Nuh feel nuh way, yuh know mi love yuh, nuff big up.

Afua Cooper

Table of Contents

Utterances and Incantations
Women, Poetry, and Dub in the Black Diaspora

This is the first anthology of its kind and it is long overdue. In these pages eleven female dub poets share their poetry with the rest of the world and one another. Dub poetry has become part of the Caribbean and International poetry landscape, and women dub poets have contributed vastly to this project, bringing their unique perspectives, riddims, words, songs, and incantations to it. It is not that women dub poets have not had access to print. Most of the women presented here have published several volumes of poetry and other kinds of literature, and all have been included in diverse anthologies, but here they come together in a single volume.

Because of the multiple sources from which dub poetry sprang, it continues to elude a neat and rigid definition. Dub poetic form originated in Jamaica. It is strongly influenced by reggae music, and also draws from other aspects of African Caribbean oral tradition, for example, proverbs, riddles, nursery rhymes, hymns, and ring games songs. In addition, and of great significance, Jamaican Creole is the *natural* language of dub poetry. Dub poetry is therefore both a poetic genre and a musical genre. Because of the reggae influence, dub poets traditionally have privileged reggae music, but jazz, rhythm and blues, calypso, African drumming styles, rap, and Afro-Latin styles have also been used by many dub poets, in the production and performance of their work. The inclusion of these forms underscores dub poetry's open-endedness, flexibility, vast potential and possibilities.

As a poetic genre, dub poetry is infused with various political and social agendas, with themes such as black liberation and the struggles of the poor being of fundamental concern to the poets. Dub poetry began as, and remains, *rebel* poetry.

Dub poetry emerged from the context of the early reggae era when toasters like U-Roy, I-Roy, King Stittt, and Big Youth broke new ground in the area of the spoken word, and in the music itself. They chanted their words over the dub side of the record, that is, the instrumentalised version, and in so doing created a new musical style. They also produced an innovative poetic form, for the poets who emerged as dub poets also used the dub version in the recitation and performance of their poems.

It was Oku Onoura who inspired by the 'vibes' of the deejays, seized the momentum of the music and invented the term 'dub' poetry to describe the new poetry he and others were writing and performing. Their poetry, like dub music, was subversive, revolutionary, and anti-establishment.

Oku, along with some other male dub poets—Linton Kwesi Johnson, Mikey Smith, and Mutabaruka—have been the ones usually associated with dub poetry's origination. And yet, almost from its inception, women were bringing new agendas and new voices, different sounds and riddims into dub. In 1976 Faybienne Miranda, a New York based poet who lived in Jamaica for a number of years, co-published a book of poetry with Mutabaruka. Though the term dub poetry was not then in use, Miranda was already writing from that sensibility.[1]

The two women most closely associated with the emergence of women in dub poetry are Lillian Allen and Jean Binta Breeze. In the early eighties Allen popularised dub poetry in Canada, and revolutionised the Caribbean Canadian poetry scene. She has been dubbed 'the birth mother' of Canadian dub poetry. Breeze who came out of the milieu of the Cultural Training Centre in

---

[1] Faybienne Miranda & Mutabaruka *Sun and Moon* (Kingston, Jamaica, 1976).

Kingston, Jamaica, became the leading female dub poet in that country and went on to do the same in Britain. In Trinidad, Pearl Eintou Springer was creating poetry in a similar vein, while Ahdri Zhina Mandiela and Afua Cooper's work helped to establish dub poetry in Canada. In Jamaica too, Anilia Soyinka helped affirm dub poetry presence by touring and performing with *Poets in Unity* a group of poet-actors from the Jamaica School of Drama. The inclusion of women's voices in dub poetry enlarged dub's discourse, made it more holistic, and opened up spaces for new perspectives and insightful analyses.

Louise Bennett, named by several dub poets as a great inspirator, and hailed as a forerunner of dub poetry by many, has made an immense contribution to Dub poetry. Long before dub poetry emerged as an art form, Bennett was one of the first Caribbean/New World artists to use Creole as a literary language. She wrote in Creole and published her poems and books in that language. The literati derided her for doing so, for after all, folk speech, Jamaican Creole, was not a real language but a 'bastard tongue.'[2] It was not good enough to be written down and published, and could not properly express complex thought, or so they said. Louise Bennett, an African Jamaican woman took no notice of her detractors and pressed on. She performed her poems, kept writing in Creole, and published her work. She gave legitimacy to poor people speech, to Black people talk, by actually writing it down. Today she is hailed as a pioneer, an innovator, a legend. But in the tradition of her ancestresses she is a warner, and a woman gifted with foresight and insight.

Dub poetry's flexibility and versatility as art is reflected in the multiple ways dub poets have manipulated, defined, and engaged the form. While music has become a feature of dub poetry, many poets prefer to perform *a cappella* or *ital*. Dub poets have pressed the media of film, video, dance, and theatre into service.

---

[2] Rex Nettleford in introduction to *Jamaica Labrish*, (Jamaica, Sangster's, 1966)

Perhaps, dub poetry's greatest contribution to poetry and art is that through its ambassadors, it has liberated poetry from the ivory towers, and fed it like fish and loaves, to the people. Dub poets have taken their poetry around the world. They read in prisons, cafes, parks, daycare centres, libraries, schools, universities, old folks homes, dance halls, night clubs, theatres, at music festivals, poetry festivals, rallies, marches, demonstrations, and on international concert stages. Dub poetry has established itself as a poetic genre that has mass appeal and women have been in the vanguard of this poetry revolution.

Female dub poets have drawn on the vast oral tradition left them by their foremothers, many of whom we may not describe as poets, but who work in the realm of the word. In the areas of folk culture, religion, and metaphysics, Caribbean women spoke with a loud voice. Women were Kumina, Myal, and Pocomania leaders. They were the mothers of Orisha worship, Condomble, Shango Baptists, and Shouters. In these spaces women were warners, ministers, shepherds, mothers, singers, drummers and poets. In the area of metaphysics—Voudou, hoodoo, root doctoring, and obeah—women were in their element. These jobs required one to have an intimate relationship with the word, for a correct and crucial use of the word was required in order to have a successful outcome.

Specifically, one such foremother is the legendary Queen Nanny. An Akan Jamaican Maroon priestess leader, anti-slavery fighter, Black liberation warrior and strategist, and renowned sorceress, she often relied upon, and used words to beat down the British babylonian slavery system that sought to destroy her and her people. Women dub poets see Nanny as an inspirator, and often invoke her in their poetic productions.

Many of us New World diasporic women know of a woman who is a competent obeah worker, a powerful warner, a gifted preacher, a strong singer, an engaging storyteller, and a talented psychic. There are stories in my family of one of my grandmothers who in addition to being a gifted singer, was also a four-eye woman. That meant that she could foretell events, see into the future. Her 'gifts' came to her through dreams. She would get up in the morning, after a dream, and begin her day with prayer. Then she would rise up and sing and sing. Whatever her dream instructed her to do that day she would do; if the message in the dream was for someone else, she would promptly deliver the message. Her children, who told me these stories, were always amazed at the accuracy of their mother's dreams. They attributed her gifts to her prayers and her intimate connection to her God. "My mother was a praying women," one of my aunts told me.

I remember growing up in the village of Whithorn in Westmoreland and being regularly awakened in the early hours of the morning by the voice of a warner as she passed by my house on her journeying. I knew she would be accompanied by a few of her relatives, and she would have a torch in her hand, lighting her path. Her voice rose in the dark morning like the ringing of a bell. God had sent her to warn the villagers (or a particular villager) of their wrongs toward a person, a family, the community, or God-self. Sometimes the warner had an inkling of "sudden death" and walked the village road shouting "sudden death, sudden death, a sudden death in the district". I would lie in my bed, afraid, because I knew her message had prophetic implications; afraid that the death would happen in my family. The warner woman would also sing sad songs, dirges, and lamentations.

If Reggae music is usually associated with dub poetry, Jamaican Creole, or Nation Language is the privileged language used by most dub poets. When dub poetry exploded on the scene it did so in Jamaican Creole, and dubbists have traditionally privileged Creole over English. One male dub poet once stated that he not only writes in Creole, but thinks in Creole also. He affirms that he does not want to write in English at all. He abhors English because it has been and still is the language of the downpresser, a language forced on him in captivity.[3] (Considered from this point of view, English becomes the bastard tongue). This is not to say that Dub poets do not write in so-called standard English. Far from it, as some poems in this collection testify. At the same time, even in 'English' poems, forms of Jamaican orature (aspects of Creole culture) appear. For example, in Afua Cooper's "The Child is Alive," the poet invokes Nanny, and celebrates the wisdom of her four-eye foremothers. But because dub poetry is *rebel* poetry, then Creole as the language of the poor, the downtrodden, those who continue to resist and resist and resist, naturally becomes the language of choice, conscious or otherwise.[4]

And these poets write using the varied and different forms of Creole available to them. From the hot tar, urban vernacular of Rae Town, Kingston, to the rural yam dialect of the hill country of Dias, Hanover or the rain-splattered Blue Mountain speech of House Hill, Portland, to a vernacular strongly inflected with urban Canada's speech patterns. Rastafari speech, as is also the case in reggae music, has made a great impact on Jamaican Creole. Naturally, Dub poetry reflects this with its poets consciously using 'dread talk.' Many dub poets are also Rastas, ex-Rastas, (though as one dread once remarked that there can be no 'X in I'), or simply write from a Rasta (chanting down Babylon) view point.[5]

---

[3] In personal conversation with Mutabaruka

[4] Jamaican poet Pam Mordecai, in conversation with this writer, once remarked that English is the language of her head, and Creole the language of her heart. She stated that when she wants to express the rumblings, sighs, and lovecries of her person, Creole presents itself as the language of choice.

[5] It is important to note that there is not one kind of Jamaican Creole or nation language, but several. In areas with strong African influences as in Eastern St. Thomas, Southern Hanover, and in Maroon communities, the dialects spoken tend to be more "rootsy".

What do women dub poets write about? Political and social themes, like slavery, colonialism, Black liberation and the plight of the poor, have been primary concerns of dub poets. Female poets, in addition to writing about these topics, have expanded dub's repertoire to include familial and women's concerns. Some have done so with a feminist stamp. Sexism, women's oppression, and liberation have all been made central to dub poetry's discourse by its female poets. These poets have expanded the definition of the term 'political' to include personal, private, and domestic matters. Women dubbists also write about love, sex, sexuality; and spirituality, healing, and women's inner life.

In addition, metropolitan poets have brought another perspective to dub poetry by dubbing down white supremacy and some of its manifestation: poor and inadequate housing for Blacks and other minority groups, marginalisation of Black youths and Black males, the exploitation of the Black woman domestic worker, the high drop-out rate of Black students within the school system, and the police murdering of Black men.

Our poetic vision is expansive. In Canada for example, dub poets as cultural workers and activists have formed alliances with other oppressed groups like the First Nations or Native peoples. Thus the poetry of the female poets also reflect our working, and solidarity, with these communities.

The women in this volume all use multiple forms that include the form of 'classical dub,' that is, a form employing chorus, and metered rhymed verses. I believe, these women poets, are more exploratory than their male counterparts, allowing their tongues to speak and their hands to write in myriad ways.[6]

---

[6] Many dub poets now move within a interdisciplinary context giving rise to a new interpretation of their work, and of dub poetry itself. Dub poetry has moved beyond its own confines leading one commentator to call it 'meta-dub.' Carolyn Cooper, *Noises in the Blood, Orality, Gender, and the "Vulgar" Body of Jamaican Popular Culture* (Durham: Duke University Press, 1995).

These artists are consummate performers. The attention they give to having their poems published and recorded balances nicely the dialectic between the written and spoken word. mandiela once did a series of performance called 'page to stage,' and the production of her *dark diaspora...in dub*, a choreo-dub poem, with its emphasis on theatre and dance, marked the beginning of a new era in dub poetry.

Nor does the 'balance between the written and spoken word' refer to a simplistic dichotomy between print and voice. A very oral poem, as in the case of Majeeda's "Daddy," is often written down and published in a book. Therefore what is oral often becomes scribal, the two forms merging into one another.

These women and other dub poets, in their journeyings with both the written and spoken word are acting out the injunction given in the chapter or *sura* "Iqra" in the Quran. In the first verse of this sura, given to Prophet Muhammad by the angel Gabriel, humanity is exhorted to: "read (recite, utter, or proclaim) in the name of thy Lord and Cherisher, who created thee from a clot, who created the use of the pen, to teach you, teach you what you know not." The believer is commanded to both "recite and write." Here, the word, the sound, and the pen are given equal attention and respect. The dub poets, messengers of the spirit and word, practise this divine command.

This spirit of triumph is at the core of the work of these female dub poets. As wordmistresses they use their language and performance to beat down a system that oppress them, their psychic selves, their well-being, their families, their kinfolk. Their poetry is both a call to arms and a sounding of the drums of victory.

It is also a call to enter the healing place. The place of the spirit is a central concern and theme for most of these eleven poets. Breeze's "Homecoming (One)", reveals the quest for a place where they can find the balm in Gilead. Women are concerned about their spiritual lives, not just in a religious sense, though that is present too. These poets recognise the need for balance in their lives, for the inner and outer to work together. It seems to me that Cherry Natural's practice of the martial arts—an integration of mind, body, and spirit—is an inner/outer quest for harmony in an inharmonious world, especially a world which constantly assaults Black people.

The poets, like the late Peter Tosh, also recognise that 'there can be no peace until we have equal rights and justice,' and so the cry they raise is at the same time a war chant and a peace offering; a love cry and a cry for justice. Their poetic utterances are like the dance of Kali, who incensed at the treatment of women and children in the world, danced her terrible dance of destruction. Out of this chaos emerged a new world of harmony, love, and order. Likewise, Demeter wandered the world weeping and looking for her daughter Persephone who was stolen from her. As nurturer of the earth, Demeter held back her bounty, causing the plants to shrivel up, the rivers to run dry, the animals and humans to cease bearing offspring, until she found her daughter. When she did, she re-established order in the world.

I would contend that these women poets are not only acting Kali- and Demeter-like, but are constantly striving to be like Maat, the Kemetic (ancient Egyptian) deity of order, harmony, balance, justice, compassion, and righteousness.

Eleven poets are featured in this volume: Lillian Allen, amuna baraka, Michelle Barrow, Louise Bennet, Jean Breeze, Afua Cooper, Queen Majeeda, Cherry Natural, ahdri zhina mandiela, Deanne Smith, and Anita Stewart aka Anilia Soyinka. These women live and work in different countries of the Atlantic World and thus come to dub poetry with different perspectives—perspectives shaped by the political, socio-cultural, and economic environments in which they live. All are Afro-diasporic. Seven live in Canada, a country that seems especially blessed with dub women. This can be partially explained by the explosion of dub poetry in Canada during the late seventies and early eighties.

There is also a powerful Jamaican influence on this body of

work. All the poets, with the exception of Michelle Barrow (Barbados) and amuna baraka (Canadian; Jamaican parents), are of Jamaican birth. The Jamaicanness of the volume is undoubtedly related to this fact that though there are now dub poets all over the world, dub poetry originated in Jamaica.

Though the Word sits at the centre of these women's lives and work, and they have made their mark as poets, they all are engaged in other endeavours that have some bearing on their poetry. Allen is a filmmaker, community and cultural worker, and an educator. baraka studies, and performs African dance with Toronto's *Sankofa Dance Ensemble*. Barrow is active in grassroots issues in her native Barbados, the Eastern Caribbean, and South Africa. Bennett is a veteran performer, actor, and broadcaster. Breeze is also a filmmaker, playwright, and dance choreographer. Cooper is a historian of the African diaspora, and writes fiction and non-fiction. Queen Majeeda is an accomplished actor, and gives poetry and acting workshops. mandiela has created a dub theatre in Canada, where she is also a respected playwright and director. She has recently ventured into filmmaking. Natural has several Black belts in various branches of the martial arts, and is active in the Jamaican women's movement. Deanne Smith is active in African drum theatre, and works also as a youth counsellor. And Stewart is an educational psychologist, and drama instructor. All of these poets have recorded their work and all use the performance as an integral part of their poetry. All have had their poems published in books and anthologies. Several have won literary and music awards.

Enjoy, then, these offerings, gifts, praises, these dirges, morningsongs, evensongs, lovesongs, prayers, thanks, revelations, invocations, these spirit possessions, this call to arms, these chants, these utterances and incantations, as these women speak to you in 'multiplying tongues.'

Afua Cooper, Toronto, Spring 1999.

Louise Bennet — Miss Lou

Louise Bennett—writer, actress, authority on Jamaican folklore—is the Hon. Louise Bennett-Coverley, O.J., affectionately known as Miss Lou. A contributor of critical importance in the development of Jamaican culture, she was awarded the Order of Jamaica in 1974. Other honours she has received include the Norman Washington Manley Award for Excellence (1972), the Musgrave Gold Medal of the Institute of Jamaica (1979) and an Honourary D. Litt, from the University of the West Indies (1983). She is the author of *Jamaica Labrish* (1966), *Anancy and Miss Lou* (1979) and *Selected Poems* (1982), each of them published by Sangster's Book Stores, Kingston, Jamaica. She resides in Toronto with her husband.

Dutty Tough
(The ground is hard)

"Rain a-fall but dutty-tuff"— wages rise but
so do prices and the cost of living.

Sun a-shine but tings noh bright,
Doah pot a-bwile, bickle noh nuff,
River flood but water scarce yaw,
Rain a-fall but dutty tuff!

Tings so bad, dat now-a-days wen
Yuh ask smaddy how dem do,
Dem fraid yuh tek i tell dem back
So dem noh answer yuh!

Noh care omuch we dah-work fa
Hard time still eena we shut,
We dah-fight, Hard-Time a-beat we,
Dem might raise we wages but —

One poun gwan awn pon we pay, an
We noh feel noh merriment,
For ten poun gwan on pon we food
Ah ten poun on we rent!

Salfish gawn up! mackerel gawn up!
Pork an beef gawn up same way,
Ah wen rice an butter ready,
Dem jus go pon holiday!

Cloth, boot, pin and needle gawn up,
Ice, bread, taxes wata-rate!
Kersene ile, gasolene, gawn up
An de poun devaluate!

De price o' bread gawn up so high
Dat we haffe agree,
Fe cut we y'eye pon bread an all
Tun dumpling refugee!

An all dem mawga smaddy weh
Dah-gwan like fat is sin,
All dem-deh weh dah fas' wid me,
Ah lef dem to dumplin!

Sun a-shine an pot a-bwile, but
Tings noh bright, bickle noh nuff!
Rain a-fall, river dah flood, but
Wata scarce an dutty tuff!

Bans O' Ooman

On the launching of the Jamaican Federation of Women for women
of all classess —"high and low, miggle and suspended..."

Bans o' ooman! Bans o'ooman!
Pack de place from top to grung
Massa lawd, me never know sey
So much ooman deh a Tung!

Up a de step and dung de passage
Up de isle and dung de wall
Not a Sunday-evening Hope tram
Pack like St. George Hall.

De ooman dem tun out fe hear
How Federation gwan.
Me never se such diffrent grade an
Kine o' ooman from me bawn.

Full dress, half dress, tidy — so-so
From bare y'eye to square-cut glass,
High an low, miggle, suspended,
Every different kine o' class.

Some time dem tan so quiet, yuh
Could hear a eye-lash drop,
An wen sinting oversweet dem,
Lawd, yuh want hear ooman clap—

Me was a-dead fe go inside
But wen me start fe try,
Ooman queeze me, ooman push me,
Ooman frown an cut dem y'eye

Me tek me time an crawl out back
Me noh meck no alarm,
But me practice bans o' tactics
Till me ketch up a platform.

Is dat time me se de ooman dem
Like varigated ants,
Dem face a-bus wid joy fe sey,
"At las' we get we chance."

Ef yuh ever hear dem program!
Ef yuh ever hear dem plan!
Ef yuh ever hear de sinting
Ooman gwine go do to man!

Federation boun to flourish,
For dem got bans o' nice plan
An now dem got de heart an soul
Of true Jamaican ooman.

Bans A Killin

So yuh a de man me hear bout!
Ah yuh dem seh dah teck
Whole heap a English oat seh dat
Yuh gwine kill dialec!

Meck me get it straight, Mas Charlie,
For me no quite understan —
Yuh gwine kill all English dialec
Or jus Jamaica one?

Ef yuh dah equal up wid English
Language, den wha meck
Yuh gwine go feel inferior when
It come to dialec?

Ef yuh cyaan sing 'Linstead Market'
An 'Water come a me yeye'
Yuh wi haffi tap sing 'Auld lang syne'
An 'Coming through de rye'.

Dah language weh yuh proud a,
Weh yuh honour an respec —
Po Mas Charlie, yuh no know seh
Dat it spring from dialec!

Dat dem start try fi tun language
From de fourteen century —
Five hundred years gawn an dem got
More dialec dan we!

Yuh wi haffi kill de Lancashire,
De Yorkshire, de Cockney,
De broad Scotch and de Irish brogue
Before yuh start kill me!

Yuh wi haffi get de Oxford Book
A English Verse, an tear
Out Chaucer, Burns, Lady Grizelle
An plenty a Shakespeare!

When yuh done kill 'wit' an 'humour',
When yuh kill 'variety',
Yuh wi haffi fine a way fi kill
Originality!

An mine how yuh dah read dem English
Book deh pon yuh shelf,
For ef yuh drop a 'h' yuh mighta
Haffi kill yuhself!

Lillian Allen

Lillian Allan is a recognised artistic figure on the Canadian cultural scene. An extraordinary poet and writer, she is one of the birth mothers of dub poetry. Often performing and lecturing internationally, Allen is the winner of two Juno awards for her recordings of poetry with music, *Revolutionary Tea Party* (1986) and *Conditions Critical* (1988). Her work includes a recording for children and young people; *Nothing But A Hero*, three books specially geared to young audience: *Why Me, Nothing But a Hero* and *If You See Truth*.

Her second collection of poetry, *Women Do This Every Day* was published in 1993 by the Women's Press, Toronto, to wide acclaim. Allen's poetry has appeared in several dozen magazines and publications internationally and in Canada and in curricula and textbooks from kindergarten through university. She is also a writer of plays and short fiction and currently teaches creative writing (part time) at the Ontario College of Art and Design.

Lillian Allen is a creative artist who has also tackled the medium of film, co-producing and co-directing *Blak Wi Blakk...* a film on Rastafarian reggae dub poet Mutabaruka. She has just released her fourth major recording project of dub poetry with music, *Freedom and Dance.*

Photograph by: Amy Gottlieb

Tribute To Miss Lou

Heartbeat
Pred out yuself Miss Lou
Lawd, yu mek wi heart pound soh
yu mek wi just love up wiself
an talk wi talk soh

spirit words
on a riddim fire
word flame beat
pumps de heart
pulses history's heat

She writes
the heartbeat of our lives
dignity/culture/politics/history/lovingness/soul
dis dressup oman wi shinning star

History
Her story
my story
his story
our story
brukout story

The Voice
The voice
strug ug ugg uggling
to be heard
hear dis;

dem sey we sey she sey he sey hear sey
raw rim of soul
her mirror a poem
with room to grow

Language
Get up
dance clap
sweat pon de ground
tambourine
sing a ring ding
sing a ring ding

If wi caant sing wi 'Linstead Market'
an 'Wata Com A Mi Yeye'
is what mek you gwine think
we coulda did feel satisfied

the language of the people
is the language of life

Wings
She gives voice
            (and)   form
                 (and)   wings to the silenced

Bear Up
Candy Seller
how is business nowadays?
A South Parade Peddle   meddle
Problems   Problems
Hardtimes

Invasions
My Dreams
see *Jamaica Elevate*
Changes
bear up people for the *Victory Parade*
It Wut It   *It Wut It*

Cho Mon
when Auntie Roachie speak
cho mon
oonu know sey if a noh soh
a near soh

A True
And the first and last sentence
in the book of her life reads:
Jamaican people in dem free spiritedness
in dem purity
in dem Caribbeaness
in dem Blackness
in dem cunning and industriousness
in dem 'tuppidness and imperfection
is precious

and even the ugliest among us
agents of doom and exploitation
you will hear say;
'A true mon. A true ting Miss Lou a talk, yes!'
Soul Flicker
Sometimes, sometimes
in the midst of oppression
a soul emerges

in the dense silence
in the conspiracy of normalcy
and officialdom

sometimes in this dimness
a flicker
a light
a path
a Miss Lou

Mrs

In the waiting room
a routine checkup
a technician came in
called me by what
she made my name
Mrs
I didn't answer but knowing
it was I, mumbled
and made my way
in a pace of my own
in a tempo earned
from struggle and long places
of silences
I no longer engage words
or meanings such as
Mistress Miss Mrs Missus

Mistress
rhymes with distress

Miss
missed nothing

Mrs
misses rarely with words

Missus
miss us, ourselves
when we answer to words
others name us

Riddim An' Hardtimes
(A dub poem)

An' Him chucks on some riddim
an' yu hear him say
      riddim an' hardtimes
      riddim an' hardtimes

Music a prance
Dance ina head
Drumbeat a roll
Hot like lead
Mojah Rasta gone dread
Natt up Natt up
irie
Red red
Riddim a pounce wid a purpose
Truths an' Rights
Mek mi hear yu

Drum
Drum Drum
Drum beat
Heart beat
Pulse beat
Drum

Roots wid a Reggae resistance
Riddim
Noh dub them call it

An' Him chucks on some riddim
an' yu hear him say
Riddim an' Hardtimes
Riddim an' Hardtimes

Dem a pounce out the music
carve out the sounds
Hard hard hard
hard like lead

But this ya country hard eh?
Ah wey we come ya fa?
Dread times
Jah signs

Drum beat
drum beat
Riddim an' hardtimes
riddim an' hardtimes

Rub A Dub Style Inna Regent Park

Monday morning broke
news of a robbery
Pam mind went
couldn't hold the load
dem took her to the station
A paddy wagon
Screaming…
her Johnny got a gun
from an ex-policeman
Oh Lawd, Oh Lawd Oh Lawd eh ya
a wey dis ya society a do
to wi sons

Rub a dub style
inna Regent Park
mon a dub it inna dance
inna Regent Park
oh lawd oh lawd

"forget yu troubles and dance"
forget yu bills them
an irie up yuself
forget yu dreams gathering dusts
on the shelves
dj rapper hear im chant
pumps a musical track
for im platform
cut it wild
sey de system vile
dubbing it inna dance

frustration pile
a different style
inna regent park

could have been a gun
but's a mike in his hand
could've been a gun spilling out the lines
but is a mike
      is a mike
            is a mike
Oh Lawd Oh Lawd Oh Lawd

riddim line vessel im ache
from im heart outside
culture carry im past
an steady im mind
man tek a draw an feeling time
words cut harsh
explanations
de sufferings of de times

"forget yu troubles and dance"
forget yu bills dem
an irie up yu self
forget yu dreams gatherin
dust   dust   dust

is a long time wi sweating here
is a long time wi waiting here
to join society's rites
is a long time wi beating down yu door

is a long time since we mek the trip
cross the Atlantic
on the slave shippppppppp
is a long time wi knocking
an every time yu slam the door
sey: no job
discrimination-injustice
a feel the whip lick
an is the same boat
     the same boat
         the same boat
Oh Lawd   Oh Lawd   Oh Lawd eh ya

dj chant out cutting it wild
sey one hav fi dub it inna different style
when doors close down on society's rites
windows will pry open
in the middle of the night
dashed hopes run wild
in the middle of the night
Oh Lawd   Oh lawd   Oh Lawd   eh ya

So What
(Perspective Poem)

So what so what so what
So your years of schooled craft
have created fine poems
so it ended pollution
so it stopped wars
so it fed starving children
so it gave life to the dying
so it brought peace to one single land
so no one should imperil its form
so if you're high up in a poetic fiefdom
so, so self assured and turgid
so what if I write a poem like a song

amuna baraka-clarke

amuna baraka-clarke helped to revive the black poetry scene in Montreal while still a teenager. She performed throughout the city and made poetry a credible staple in cultural and political circles. In addition to hosting the television program *Black is...* she was also featured in special radio segments of the program *Poetic Response*. As the words of poets began to spread through Montreal she began to take on larger projects and in 1991 the birth of **dap** (diasporic afrikan poets) became a reality.

The group performed throughout Montreal and networked with poets from other parts of the country. It was her first meeting with adrhi zhina mandiela that opened her eyes to the lyrical possibilities of writing in Jamaican Nation language. While amuna has woven her words thru many video, print and oral media, it was her participation in Toronto's International Dub Poetry Festival in 1993 that left an indelible mark on the young writer. amuna's art takes on many forms, but the rhythm and the beauty of patwa engulfs her and has naturally influenced her writing styles. Her move to Toronto and participation in the poetry scene has given her the opportunity to grow.

In addition to having her work published in *Fireweed* and *At The Crossroads* she had the opportunity to edit the poetry and fiction content of the latter. Currently she dances with the Sankofa Dance and Drum Ensemble, and serves on the board of directors for both the Black Coalition for AIDS Prevention and b current. This woman of the diaspora says that she is simply striving to leave the world more beautiful than she inherited it.

Photograph by: Cleveland Joseph

2nite

2nite
as dih lights dim
i wonder where u are
as the air chills
i dream of u still
wishing you werent so far

i watch the couples on the street
as they lovingly retreat
but whose arms will hold me now
yesterday
everyday
monday tuesday
to sunday
in my thoughts u remain
& now

i cd use a likkle love 2nite
as dih sun disappears
& dih moon shines bright
i cd use a likkle love 2nite
a likkle love 2nite

independent
though i know i be
yr touch cd serve me well
i dont need u
i tell myself
still my heart tells a different tale

as i move into my bed
i know what lies ahead
a passion made for two
i retreat
into my sheets
hand & centre they do meet
cant deny in my sleep
how i do
(really)

want a likkle love 2nite
as dih sun disappears
& dih moon shine bright
i cd use a likkle love 2nite
a likkle hug 2nite
a likkle kiss 2nite
a likkle warmth 2nite
a likkle chat 2nite
cd use yr love 2nite …
        i cd use a likkle u
                2nite

reggae sistrength

i wanted 2b in a reggae band
interlocked wid riddims of mih sistren
i wanted to create new stylies
                new vibrations
& jus level some cool vibes

i wanted 2b in a female reggae band
& mek a joyful noise unto dih island posse
   & sistren massive
& jus pulse libations to the ancestors

i wanted to
   wanted to
      i did want to
travel dih world
delivering messages of love to one people
but
   mih know seh
      hotels are not good homes 4 children
& its hard to separate dih white from dih color
prepare ital dinners evry night
& keep dih house tidy
   between sound checks

i wanted 2b in an all female reggae band
& make my body become one wid de dub
but mih never did know a man who wd (like rita)
wait 2 envelop me in fih im ebony arms
after mih share mih love wid dih world
i wanted 2b in a woman's reggae group
but fih we group don't survive
as we family, lover, & friend
bind we down
& nuh set we free

mih mudda tongue

fus of all
mih haffi big up dih island massive
& dih sistren posse
one love & nuff respect to u who
did take dih time to see me thru
all mih irie incantations
& big up to alla weh bahn ah faw-rehn
& still cling to a place call back ome

i've always wanted to do that
always wanted to speak 2u thru
words of resistance
pokomania
creole
rastafari
patwa
caribbean nation language

always wanted to liberate my tongue
from
my canadian downbringing
wanted 2b able to
get inside mih tongue
&
speak dih speak
of land we from
mek dih riddim in mih soul tek control
mek dih movement of my lips
memba dih journey pan slave ships
in mih soul

what i really want to say is
mih waan back mih tongue
(but i was born in canada)
mih seh mih waan back me tongue
(i'm not ja-fake-an)
mih waan fih speak 2u thru the talking blues
mih waan fih live & love
thru jah's blessings from above
waan dih old folks talk
fih live with legitimacy

i hear mih voice
tryin to rise above the noise
mih jus ah hear dih sound
jus a batta all around
mih sey mih hear a cry
gwan mek dih colonizer die
in me

& now mih mek a choice
hear jamaican in mih voice
& i can feel it pound
want to scream & chat it loud
mih bid dih english bye bye
cuz patwa a mih destiny

go away mih sey gwey
come here mih sey come yeh
feel dih nation language
jus a tek hold ah mih
what a boonoonoonoos guy
dem sey damn he looks fly

mek we dweet/let us do it
a nuh nuttin/nothing to it
mih a guh learn what fih do
(if mih even haffi call miss lou)
watch me chant
       see mi chant
              hear i chant

mih seh mih waan back mih tongue

trial & tribulation

blk ooman
tribulation suffering
blk ooman
trouble wid yr loving
blk ooman
why ah always u haffi fine dih way
fih mek tings right

smaddy tell me why
mih mudda always had to be dih one
to mek dih peace

smaddy tell me why
we lovah haffi scorn we
university degree

smaddy tell me why
mih sistren all alone

haffi raise kids on ar own
wid no one to depend on
wid no one to lend one
hand

blk ooman
tribulation suffering
blk ooman
trouble wid yr loving
blk ooman
why ah always u haffi find dih way
to compromise

everyday it seem
mih aunty ride dih subway
while de res ah we still sleep

everyday it seem
blk men dem jus ah use we
tell we body feel so weak

everyday it seem
we facing exploitation
always undah someone knee
it feel like
it never ending
wid no one ever sendin aid

blk ooman
tribulation suffering
blk ooman
trouble wid yr loving

blk ooman
why ah always we
haffi fine dih way
why ah always we
haffi mek dih way
why ah always
    we
haffi mek tings right

united colours of benneton

what a gwan benneton
what a gwan wid benneton

when i taking dih train
i see dem ads at every stop & i cry out in pain
becuz the images
of i & i
perpetuate all dem
white lies

dem seh blk is bad & white is right
all whitey look like gold
all we is blk as nite
but dat nuh right
dis sight of oppression
so stop all of dis exploitation
cuz it nuh right dese signs of downpression
mih nah 'low dem fih dis fih we blk nation

what a gwan wid benneton...

everywhere i turn
& everywhere i look
i see dem clothing ads wid jah people
scattered all aroun babylon neighbourhood

i see white goldilocks
& a blk child fox
for dat picture dem need a good box

i see blk ooman
ah nurse white baby
& dem ave dih nerve fih seh dem end slavery

& dere's a white wolf
ready fih nyam blk sheep
lawd how dem love depict we as enemy

& mih nuh understand
how dem so presumptuous
fih show a white man ah grab mih fih mek mih im lovah

what a gwan wid bennetton....boycott haffi go on!

a taste of the caribbean

there are three things i have come to learn
inspires heated debate
they be religion, politics, but worse dan dese
naming the caribbean food on yr plate

ever been enjoyin a meal
conversation flowing wid ease
when u say to dih trini whose home u are at
please to pass dih rice and peas

one hell of a singtin start den
doh we all raise fih be polite
im stare in mih face seh if you waan dih food
u mus call it peas & rice

mih seh i & i is from jam down
dih home of dih yellow, green & blk
but let's not fuss i'll have something else
i think ginnip would make a nice snack

well who would ah evah thought
is chenet dem call ginnip
den dih bahamian gal whey mih did ah sit beside said
chile let me give u a tip

what we call duff is like yr blue drawers
and we have something call coconut cake
& we give that one name to what u call drops
grater cake is another namesake

well the trini got louder & louder
and in that sing song accent dem chat wid said
by dih way when u making rice
boil it up then use a strainer to strain it

dont u know bout the dangers of starch in rice
& the pebbles u does fine in rice grain
so while it's important to pick thru yr rice
u must clean it all the same

then dis one haitian man taan up & look around
& ask fih some calloloo
but is okra im mean so mih pass him dat green
& dih trini reach fih sitten whey look like stew

& just den dih bajan pipe up
& ah sitten name cou-cou him offah
it look like dih cawnmeal we feed to we dawg
but gal mih taste it & it mek mih mout watah

eventually everyting quiet down
& mih haffi sey mih did learn a lot
bout dih similarity among island
even though the evening was hot

i did leave wid a taste of the caribbean
& learn fih mih food is not completely unique
but dih nex time i dine at smaddy house
i'll go equipped wid appropriate speech

growing up

little girl/growing up / learning of their ways
double dutch/ pat hands / numbered were those days

i long for dih days when / i likkle girl did
run thru dih grass
and feel dih breeze upon my skin
but now all i do feel / concrete grazing my feet
dere silk roses
prick & make me bleed/
ing heart white liberal friend / seh dem understan
whenever babylon
kill we & get off
but ah dem same one who
at school time used to
gwan like my nose was the biggest thing on dih face of dis eart'

young lady / nappy head /told she not as good (as dem)
soup & sandwich / fih we rice & peas / division in
we neighbourhood

gone off to big school / made to learn their rules
out of the home
of the ones who used to tell me
ten times better than / every last white man
u must be
if u want to get a head /
ing off to the job world / sure to mek mi sweat
cuz mih know the prospect
slim fih alla we

blk english ooman
white french man land
but me mus create space fih teach

blk woman / struggling hard / but she says dont play
(their game)
i met the challenge / beat the odds / culture was my way

Michelle Barrow

Michelle Barrow is a Popular Theatre Animator, Adult Educator and Poet. She sees herself as a Caribbean National born in Barbadoes. Michelle studied in Jamaica and worked throughout the Caribbean and South Africa. Her printed work includes a poem entitled "Rebellious Red" in the anthology, *So Much Poetry In We People*, published by the Eastern Caribbean Popular Theatre Organization (E.C.P.T.O) in 1988/89 and edited by Kendel Hippolyte in St. Lucia.

She currently lives in South Africa.

Rebellious Red

You told me you didn't like me wearing
lipstick
and though your reason wasn't the best
for six days I wore my lips naturally brown
This morning after we quarrelled
I painted my lips
"REBELLIOUS RED"

Here's To My Hair
(to the natural in me)

Sister you name it
I've done it!
I've fried it!
And dyed it!
Almost petrified it
greased it
teased it
Still couldn't appease it
And that time I weaved it
Girl I really grieved it.

Now I've changed
My head's been rearranged
Now I row it
And 'fro it
And I've gotten to know it

And I know it's happy
just being nappy
And bringing out the natural in me.

Untitled

I have this fear
Not a great big phobia-like fear
Yet not a fear to be ignored

A fear of always being
Auntie Shellz or god mummy, but never
Mother, ma, mama, mummy.
It is there mainly when I go home
(For I'm presently in a kind of exile)
I see them, those mothers
My sisters and friends
Beam with pride at their little "thems"
If I had little "mes"
I'd want them to be inoculated
With my grandmother's strength
Fed with my mother's gentleness
Watered with my father's tears
Me, I'd train them up in the way they should go
So when they are old
They'd not depart from it.

But I have this fear
Not a great big phobia-like fear
Yet not a fear to be ignored.

Psalming

Sing a psalm a day ma sistren
Sing a psalm a day
It will lift you up
It will make you strong
It will help you on life's rugged way

Sing a psalm a day when ya down
and ya face to the ground
but ya look up and see the hills
and remember that is God
that ya help come from
and ya know dat it always will
for if it wasn't for the Lord
on we side
now tell me, where would we be.
If it wasn't for his peace and protection
the enemy surely wudda nyam we.

Sing a psalm a day ma sistren
Sing a psalm a day
It will lift you up
It will make you strong
It will help you on life's rugged way

sing to yaself in psalms and hymns
and ting
look sing and make your heart glad
Gal, sing and dance and give thanks to the Lord
cause he's the best friend

you evah had.
Sing a psalm about righteousness
a psalm about his grace
a psalm of his compassion too
shout a psalm about his faithfulness
a psalm about his love
and his mercies toward you.

Sing a psalm a day ma sistren
Sing a psalm a day
It will lift you up
It will make you strong
It will help you on life's rugged way.

Passers Through

If you are one of those
Brave Black Brothers
Who passed through this door
this door to my heart
I salute you.
For t'was not just from the clan mothers
I gleaned and gained
The strength I have to stand
I honed these standing skills
When you ventured through my world
(and I through yours)
I learnt the cleansing power of tears
The bile-bitter taste of anger

That a simple prayer over-cometh fear
That love is a game
A circle
A song
And there's always somebody
who wants to play and win
To break and remake
to rewrite and croon
(out of time and out of tune)
ME
I learnt that this voice will not be silenced
by your kissing lips
nor your angry words
nor fear of you leaving.
Know this
That I too am brave
Enough to stand up for myself
by myself
That yes though sometimes I may be lonely
I am never alone
And so, Black man who
passed through this portal
Pass again
If you dare
Pass again.

Jean 'Binta' Breeze

Jean 'Binta' Breeze is a mother, dub poet, performance actress, dancer, choreographer, and theatrical director. She is a popular Jamaican Dub poet and storyteller whose performances are so poweful she has been called a 'one woman festival'. She was a teacher of English and Drama in her home parish of Hanover, Jamaica. She was also a cultural organizer with the Jamaican Cultural Commission and trained at the Jamaica School of Drama.

With Mutabaruka she produced her first recording *"Slip yu fool" yu neva go to African school.* Since then she has recorded *Tracks* (1996) and continues to record on numerous collections. She has published four books of poems. *Answers, Ryddim Ravings*, (Race Today, 1988), *Spring Cleaning* (Virago, 1993) and *On the Edge of an Island* (Bloodaxe Books, 1997). She has performed her work throughout the world, including tours of the Caribbean, North America, Europe, South East Asia and Africa, and now divides her time between Jamaica and London, England.

Grandfather's Dreams

His hands were
working hands
spread out on the table
they became maps
veined roads
intertwining
everything was touched
with care
these hands would free
the unseen shoots
of soft green baby leaves
would carve out land
for yams
like African sculptures
would beat time rhythmic
checking breadfruits
ready for the eating
would
in the simple doing of a task
show us all our crafting
all our art

and his eyes
his vision
held somewhere in the heavens
were like clouds
promising us
growing up on rock
much needed rain

he sat lightly
on his clay mountain
where the sun
blackbronzed his face
into golden masks of ancestors
shapes and colours changing
with each new hour of the day

the cinnamon steam
of chocolate mornings
cooled
in his coco podded hands
the midday oilsheen sweat
he wiped away
the evening coal-black cool
of his homecoming
smelling of bush
and ripening naseberries
feeding the birds he knew as well as
neighbouring families

and when the winds
drifted us
overseas
in search of dreams
in search of 'tings gettin betta'
because we could not swim to Africa
and when we did not find the
gold he never sought
just   more horizons
like he'd known, somehow,
that people do the same things everywhere

how many of us
drowned in desperate ways
Atlantic drinking in our cries
how many of us
hands now bloodied
in the factory's making
of shapes we did not dream
find our hands
with or without our knowledge
reaching for
a straw
some clay
a metal scrap
some words
to shape a moment richer
than anything we sought
and in the making
see him
pause
and look for us
over more than distance
more than time

and we
holding something sacred
in our hands
hands now mapped
from other journeys
veined with newer songs
would reach out
place it on his mantle
knowing it cost

some million heartbeat
and say
'Asante sana baba'

this is
for you

Mermaids

somewhere
along the road
a woman eases off
her load
unwraps
her bundles
smells
her desires

today
a woman comes
in ragged cloth
scratching plants
tearing leaves
head down
in grave concern
she throws herself
to water

now
on the edge
a woman cries

her rivers wide
cups a hand
and drinks

>her sisters hairs
>are in her throat
>her sisters dreams
>wake in her veins
>in swift recoil
>she curls the ground
>around her

the river whispering
wash your hair
rushes over banks
caressing

>o lover
>do not ask one more
>let her voice be wind
>as it was before
>do not bring down
>her waters

the wispy rags
fluttered dry
lashes softly opening
slipping from
her lover's arms
her thighs
stroke through
the water

her head rests
on a sunwarmed stone
she sings
in flute soft laughter
opens flowers
with a kiss
and paints her scales
in aqua

somewhere
along the road
a woman
eases off her load
unwraps
her bundles
chooses
her own fruit

Homecoming (One)

is dat day
wen yuh put yuh key
in yuh own front door
an wipe yuh foot
from de dus
of all unwelcome

settle yuh children
roun yuh table
full of good wholesome
food
an sing to dem

loud as yuh desire
but mostly sof
so dem dreams
will not be frightening

den yuh put yuh foot up
ease yuh bones
ready
to meet de dawning
of dem opening eyes

dat day
wen yuh tek awn life
an know
yuh have de will
to mek it
an a man don't mess

dat day sister
wen yuh reach over
de blues
an it don't matter
wedda outside
cowl or hot
stony or smood
high or low
for inside warm
wid all de loving
from yuh heart

dat day, sister
name
Homecoming

Warner

Thunder shattered dreams
lightning struck the vision
an de sky mek up it face
far over de distant mountain
ginger root dry up
an de needle dem fly
come hitch up on de clothesline
Madda head wrap
eena a red blood turban
inch measure roun er waist
two lead pencil
sharpen to teet point
an Natty let out a scream
from under the moon
im chantin Death
to all black and white
dungpressor

an de baby madda
clamp dung pon er stomach muscle
lack er foot tight
fah Herod sword nah come een tonight
an river nah rush no more

Madda tek pickney by de han
an de cymbal dem start sing
she sayin I
I come to bring a warnin
fah de Lawd Gad say to tell you
dat de day of your sins is upon you

dat de day of tribulation is nigh
an de Lawd Gad say to tell you
to hearken
hearken to de people dem voice
fah dem rod shall lay open de mountain
and de river
de river shall run dry

den she tun two roll
an disappear
eena de fiery chariot
wid Elijah
jus as Natty step aff de hillside
an im nah smile
nah sey peace an love no more
im look straight into the burning sun
and sey Fire an Brimstone
just wen de people start listen
one big foreign chevrolet
drive up an tek im een
an one lef in de hills a wail
sey where is im ital queen

an de baby madda
wid de heart dem a push out troo er mout
more prick unda er skin fi flush er out
kean talk
        fah if de riva mumma die
                if de riva mumma die
who shall cure the pain

Pipe Woman

stripped down dry
and smoked

eyes like precious stones
inside the folding layers
of her skin

cheeks are sucked in
deep on a wooden stem

cup held
in wiry hands

fire enters
rolls around her tongue
fills her belly
      rope into knots
she turns a dark blue black
steams up
      an yuh can see rain coming

dancing clouds
leave the cavern of her mouth
her nose
      a sign of habitation

here
between battles
she breathes guidance
beware

if she bows to drink
for them
she belches fire

Dubwise

'cool an
    deadly'
snake
    lady
writhing
    'roun
    de worlie'
    wraps
        her sinews
roun his
    pulse
        and grinds
        his pleasure
        and disgust
            into a
            one dance
        stand

to equalise
    he grins
        cockwise
            at his bredrin
        and rides
            a 'horseman scabie'

or bubbles a
   'water
      bumpie'
 into action

the d.j
  eases a
   spliff
from his lyrical
    lips
 and smilingly
   orders
 'Cease'

Riding On De Riddym

riding on de riddym a we time
sorting out the questions on we mind
wedda hustling on street corner
or white collared in de corridor
we own images we seeking to define

de cap couldn't fit
de muse pack er grip
move outa Egyp
now she roving like a gypsy
cause accomodation
it nat easy
an too much craft is reachin er by telephone
an she didn' waan go mental all alone

so she can change up er french line image
an she skankin down de frontline raw
meeting metaphors mongs King Tubby's hi fi
tappin out a timin mongs de hip hop an de jive
jumpin de A train to a Harlem song
weh words flying like bullets
baratta strong
realising how bored she had been
all long

now we riding on de riddyms a we time
sorting out de questions on we mind
wedda hustling on street corners
or white collared in de corridor
we own images we seeking to define

de Latin wasn' hip
pentecostal tongue lick we lip
light we wid poetic flame
mongs de kumina, de shango,
de ettu an de balm
everyone weh hear can understand
in de yard, in de park
in de football stan'
de muse now say she coming live
she don' like how er influence get prioritise
wid de five percent a light demself
an aestheticise
an de majority don' even realise
dat is dem retain de culture dat keep er alive
so she jump offa de page
jump on de stage

mongs de d.j. an de dancehall
de jazz, de blues, de grays,
poetry now bus out a de stays

an we riding on de riddym a we time
sorting out de questions on we mind
wedda we hustling on street corner
or white collared in de corridor
we own images we seeking to define
an de muse sey to tell yuh
she having a rapsiraggaraving time

Afua Cooper

Afua Cooper, one of Canada's most versatile poets, is of Jamaican origin. Hers is an oracular voice. She comes in the tradition of the shamaness, the warner, the four-eyed woman chanting flaming words. Afua's poetry has a strong sense of history and place, and incorporates African riddims and the musical vibes of the African Diaspora. She writes from a feminist sensibility and has published three books of poetry, the last of which *Memories Have Tongue* (Sister Vision Press, 1993) won a Casa de las Americas prize.

Her poetry has been widely anthologised and she has con- tributed to the dub poetry aesthetic both internationally and in Canada. She was one of the organisers of the First International Dub Poetry Festival held in Toronto, in the spring of 1993.

Afua is completing her doctorate in history at the University of Toronto. Her dissertation is a biographical study of African American abolitionist Henry Bibb. She is co-author of *We're Rooted Here and They Can't Pull Us Up: Essays in African Canadian Women's History* (University of Toronto Press, 1994), which won the prestigious Joseph Brant award for history.

Photograph by: James Hodgins

Birds of Paradise

At dawn my mother stands on the hill
behind our house
and invokes the sun to rise
she goes to the outdoor kitchen
and prepares tortillas and cocotea for breakfast

My mother sells fruits and flowers in the market
fruits and flowers she tends and grows
she does not have to not solicit customers
they come to her of their own volition
and at the end of each day
her items are all sold

Now at age 42 my mother decides to stop having children
"I have peopled the world with the numerous men
and women that my body has birthed," she says
"now it's time for me to birth other things"

At times my mother's back and feet grow tired
I anoint them with coconut oil
her feet a detailed map
her back the starapple tree outside our front door

My mother has never travelled abroad
but she knows tales of everyland
she says the flowers in her gardens
especially the ginger lily, orchids,
and the birds of paradise, bring her such tidings

My mother is short in stature
all her children tower above her
some do not want to recognise
or acknowledge her as they pass by in the marketplace
they are ashamed of this fruit and flower woman
this woman who fed them milk and tortillas
to make them strong
sometimes they mock her
"she looks like something out of a Rivera mural,"
but my mother does not hear
her ears are beyond their words.

In the evening when she grows weary
my mother sings lullabies to the sun to entice it to sleep
so the dark can come and we can rest
"It's in the darkness that we grow strong," she tells us

How wise she is
this woman with a life that no one can capture
how essential she is
this woman who makes gardens flower
who feeds us milk and tortillas
I watch her as she descends the hill to the marketplace
her skirt at her knee
her black hair flecked with grey

At The Centre

Today doves flew from my head
and my hair grew
the longing is gone from my body
and I'm filled with peace, perfect peace

No longer shall I speak of electrocuted poets
or the ones who inhaled gas until
they danced in the dizziness of death
But of brown women
who turn the soil with their hands
making vegetable gardens and tending fruit trees

Today I went into my storehouse
selected the finest oil and anointed my body
wrapped myself in the rarest cloth
of a deep wine red
stood at my front gate
and words poured from my mouth in flaming chants

Today the craftsman has come
to make a design for me
of a woman sitting in a deep repose
with doves flying from her head
I shall hang it at my window for all the world to see

The Child Is Alive

And a niece of granny Nanny
an Akan woman, a woman who can see far,
a woman with the knowledge of herbs
a woman who works in the field, cutting cane
a woman who speaks the language of her grandmothers
a woman who tells stories of magical animals
of talking trees, and of fabled cities beneath mighty rivers
a woman who was stolen from her village when she was 14
a woman who was raped on the slave ship by a white sailor
a woman who flies to Africa when she sleeps

This woman, this niece of granny Nanny
takes her cutlass and runs with the swiftness
of Sogolon Conde in her guise as buffalo woman
this woman runs with her machete
an ancient chant rising from her throat
an ancient chant imploring God and all the
spirits that attend women in childbirth to come
to her aid
She calls her companions
"form a circle around the dead woman
breathe, breathe deeply, give her breath,
give her life."

This woman, this niece of granny Nanny enters
the circle with her cutlass, the ancient chant
leaping from her lips,
cuts open the belly of the woman and releases the child
while her companions hum and chant softly

Oh praise the ancestors!
the child is alive
Oh Onyame, take the spirit of the mother*
praise to the ancestors,
in the midst of misery and pain
in the midst of humiliation and grief
in the midst of this inhumanity
praise to the ancestors, the child lives
Oh Onyame, take the spirit of the mother

This woman, this niece of granny Nanny,
this ancient midwife
dances with the child, backward, forward, sideward
spins and joins her companions dancing like the priestess
she would have been had not slavers stolen her away
from her people
the woman dances
east
south
west
north
she holds the child up to the sky
blessings

Oh praise to the ancestors
the child lives
Oh Onyame, take the spirit of the mother
Oh praise to the ancestors
the child is alive!
Woye! woye! woye!

*Onyame is the Twi (Akan language) for God

Woman A Wail
(A New Creation)

Chorus: Woman a wail
di eart is in labour
woman a wail
creation in danger
woman a wail
di eart is in labour
and what shall she bring forth from her travail?

Her mountains shall roar and spit fire
her bowels shall move and cause the eart to split
from one end to another
our minds too shall be rent asunder
this woman shall avenge herself

(chorus)

Who is she that looketh forth as the morning,
fair as the moon, clear as the sun,
but terrible as an army with banners*

She wail an bawl
as she destroy but
she create again and again
she wail an shriek
as she bring forth
a new way of thinking
a new way of living
a new understanding

and
a new
new
new creation

From the mouth of the Ganges
from the throat of the Yangtze
from the heart of the Niger
from the belly of the Amazon
she dance
she dance down lightning and thunder
she dance down brimstone and fire
she is a mighty earthquake
she is a non-stop hurricane
she dance
            and
                    dance
and   dance and dance
she dance down lightning and thunder
she dance down brimstone and fire, fire
she is a mighty whirlwin
she is a non-stop volcano, ooh

She dance her dance of terror
she dance her dance of fear
look she dancing on the four winds
dancing the world's end, ooh

ah seh
woman a wail
the eart is in labour

woman a wail
creation in danger
woman a wa-eh-eh-eh-eh -ail
the eart is in labour
and what shall she bring forth from her travail
what shall she bring forth from her travail?

A new way of tinking
a new way of living
a new understanding
a new way fi si tings
a new way fi do tings
and
A new Creation
A new Creation
A new Creation

*Song of Solomon, chap. 6, verse 10.

True Revolution

Revolution in wi heart
revolution in wi thought
revolution in wi house
revolution in di street
revolution widin and widout

No Kamau
there won't be a revolution because

once again dem bring in di colonisers
(Americans dis time)
to whip di people into submission

No Kamau
there won't be a revolution because
artists and other would-be revolutionaries
get loss on di fantasy ilan of cocaine
an ilie is no longer Jah holy herb

No Kamau
there won't be a revolution because
punanis rule the airwaves
an di voice of protest is weak

No Kamau
there won't be a revolution because
gold chains shackle wi necks an minds
while Black miners die (still) in South Africa

Kamau
Your name means warrior
and we need warriors like you
fi dance di martial chant
we need Far-I to sound Nyahbinghi drums
we need ones wid di spirit of Nanny and Tacky
to plan and strategise
to lay in wait and strike at di enemy
widin and widout

We need fi clean wiself
fi respect wiself

fi respect di female part of wiself
an to know
dat ooman degradation
Black ooman degradation
Black people degradation must stop

We need fi hav love fi wiself an wi neighbours
and to know that love indeed is divine
then Kamau
when all these and more tasks are completed
we will have, oh yes, we will have, we will truly have a
Revolution

Revolution in wi heart
revolution in wi thought
revolution in wi house
revolution in di street
revolution widin and widout
revolution 360 degreeeeee

Confessions Of A Woman Who Burnt Down A Town

I buried the twins that evening
they died of smallpox
only 8 months old
Madame came to the funeral
and said to me by way of consolation
'c'est la vie,
I too have lost my own.'

I went back to work
back to work in Madame's house
that same evening at supper she yell afa me
an box me full ina mi face 'cause
Mi tun ova di gravy bowl in har lap

I remember my journey from my island to this island
Rhode Island to Montreal
Lived in Rhode Island all my life 'till
monsieur came from Montreal on one of his trips
he bought me
Him seh mi look like a healthy wench.
Him ded soon afa an Madame nevah forgive me
But mi nevah have anyting to do wid it
him ded a consumption

The twins died too.
After we buried them that evening
my heart changed position in my chest
and I was seized with one burning desire
and that was to leave the prison of this island
But where could I go
because throughout the whole world
in all the continents people who look like me
were bound
But still, all mi coulda see was
mi feet running, no chain, no rope, no shackle
free

madame talking to her best friend
and confessor Father Labadie —
I'm going to sell that negress, she's getting too uppity

And furthermore since François died
I just can't seem to manage
Look a buyer for me father, perhaps the church?
I bring in the food an pretend like ah neva hear
an serve the food good and proper
was on my best behaviour
roll back mi lip and skin mi teeth
roll back my yai and show the white
den I went back to mi room in the cellar
and mek mi plan

Smoke, smoke, too much smoke
only intend fi one house fi burn
fire, fire, too much fire
but it done go so already
and I running
my feet unshackled, unbound,
free
running pass di city limits
while behind me di fire rage
and my raging heart change back
into its rightful position

He was running too
an apprentice, from France
I gave him all my food to take me or show me
the way to New England but he tek the food
and leave me while I was sleeping
an the constables caught me

I don't utter a word as I sit in the jailhouse
Father Labadie come to confess me

but I refuse
their god is not my god
"Arson is one of the worst crimes in New France Marie,"
he say to me, "confess now and save your soul."
I spit on the ground
outside, the mob wants to rip me from limb to limb
but mi nuh fraid, a strange calm fill mi body
and I'm at peace, peace, perfect peace

Guilty, the judge pronounced
and the sentence: to be tortured, my hands cut off
my body burned and the ashes scattered
to the four corners of the earth
Mi bruk down, mi body crumple ina heap
Before mi yeye mi see mi twins
An dem look so alive as if dem jus
waitin fi mi come nurse dem
Dem reduce the sentence
Now I am to be hanged only and my body burned
Father Labadie come back for di confession
And I confess
is I Marie who set the fire
I say yes
I start it in madame's house by de river
50 building destroy
the hospital, the cathedral
I confess
is I Marie who burn dis city
so write that down Father Labadie
write down my story so it can be known in history
with my heart burning I tek di sacrament
and accept di final rites

outside di guard is waiting
to tek me to di hangman's noose
Soon I will be free from di prison of dis island
an I will fly an fly an fly

Memories Have Tongue

My granny seh she have a bad memory
when I ask her to tell me some of her life
she seh she can't rememba much
but she did memba di 1910 storm
an how dem house blow down
an she had to go live wid her granny
down at bottom house

She her memory bad
but she memba dat when her husband died
(both of dem were thirty)
she had t'ree likkle children
one in her womb
one in her arms
an one at her frocktail

She memba when dem bury him
her heart jus bussup inside
dat when di baby bawn
she no have no milk in ar breas

She memba how she wanted her dawta
to grow up an be a postmistress

but di dawta died when she was likkle
an she point to di croton-covered grave
at di bottom of di yard

She seh her memory bad
but she memba 1938
Frome
di riot
Busta an
Manley
but what she memba mos of all
is dat a pregnant woman was shot an killed
by di soldiers

Chile, I ole now
mi brain gaddarin water
but I memba as a young woman, I love to dance
an yellow was my favourite colour
It was my husban fadda
who ask fi mi han
di big people dem siddung outta hall
an discuss everyting
my fadda agree cause he said
my fellow, your granfadda
was 'an honourable person'

I memba too how on my wedding day
mi relatives dem nearly eat off all di food
it was alright, doah
I was too nervous to eat anyway

Queen
Majeeda

Queen Majeeda — Born Karlene Hamilton on October 3, 1968 in St. Andrew, Jamaica, she attended Merl Grove High School and the University of the West Indies School of Continuing Studies, where she pursued Small Business Management. She completed a Creative Writing course at the University of the West Indies and is now a student at the Edna Manley College of the Visual and Performing Arts where she is pursuing Acting, Voice and Speech.

She produced her first single *Oh Daddy* which was released in 1991 in Jamaica and her debut CD *Conscious*, also produced by her, was released in 1993 by the Massachusetts based record company HEARTBEAT RECORDS. She recently released another self produced single *Modern Day Slavery* and is working on her manuscript of poetry. Queen Majeeda has been twice nominated for the Jamaican Music Award in the category of Female Dub Poet in 1995 and 1996.

Photograph by: Kay Westhues

Oh Daddy

Oh daddy, oh daddy
Where are you?
Oh where are you?

I look around
What do I see?
Children chasing their daddy
For books and school shoes, lunch money
Oh where are you running to, dear daddy?
You must share the responsibility
And don't leave de whole a it pon mommy

Oh daddy, oh daddy
Where are you?
Oh where are you?

Children crying oh mommy
Oh where, oh where is our daddy
You one can't manage nine a we
Now you tell dis to our daddy
School start back and him nuh pay we school fee
And everyday we go a school without lunch money

Oh daddy, oh daddy
Where are you?
Oh where are you?

Oh look sista dat's our daddy
Him come to look for we and mommy

Good evening daddy what you bring for we?
I don't have nutt'n go ask yu mommy

Oh daddy, oh daddy
Where are you?
Oh where are you?

Nine months pass and we nuh see no daddy
But what we see is another baby
Oh no mommy, not another one a we!
You can't manage ten a we
Now you hear dis anywhey yuh deh daddy
Mommy one can't mind ten pikney

Oh daddy, oh daddy
Where are you?
Oh where are you?

Our Glorious Past

There was a time when we walked this earth
With such glory, such dignity
We were in our own land
We were kings and queens
Princes and Princesses
We held our heads high
We were noble, a royal nation
Ours was a land civilized
So civilized we ruled with each other

and not over each other.
        There was religious liberty
In the land of nobility
Till the raiders came
And forced unto us what they call Christianity.
        And our history?
We wrote our own history
And told our own stories
It was as we lived it
        We gave civilization to this world
We gave art, science and literature too
But what have we gotten in return?
        We were robbed
We fell into the hands of thieves
They hold today what we had yesterday
This exchange was not our plan
Why did we become servants, when we were once rulers?
Why are strangers now our masters?

Remember now our history
Way, way beyond slavery
We ruled in our own society
Remember now, lest we forget
Don't say the Middle Passage journey was too horrifying
        too long
To remember where we are coming from
And think ourselves mere descendants of slaves
Forgetting the legacy our ancestors gave
A culture so rich was to be passed on
To Africa's children, heirs to many thrones
So many kingdoms, yet we were not divided

The land was ours
The food and the resources it provided
     Medical science and astronomy
Were all part of this legacy
This is where our roots lie
In things noble and dignified
We have to go back to our roots
Find out for ourselves what is truth
We no longer accept your lies
Bury them because the truth must rise
A civilized nation did not come
And find a nation of savages
Savages instead came and found a civilized nation
And stole what we had for documentation
But they could not destroy our oral tradition.

    We found what we have lost
What was lost was stolen
The history of our glorious past
    We have found it
And now we reclaim
    It's ours.

Modern Day Slavery

Tax increase, price increase
Strike, strike and more strike
Due to high cost of living and low pay

But is what a gwaan in a dis ya country?
Me seh a nutt'n but chaos in a we society
Yu tek a bus is a Middle Passage journey
Wuk like farmer horse still we can't see no money
To me dis look like modern day slavery
'Ca after yu rush out a yu yard so early
Wuk all day plus overtime fe earn more money
By de time yu reach home yu so tired
Yu can't even spend likkle time wid yu family
Not to mention yu drop asleep while talking to the Almighty
You tell me if dat a nuh modern day slavery?

Food price climb so high we can't reach it
Light bill and water bill a mock we salary
Look how de system enslave we
A how we a go free out a dis ya modern day slavery?
And de leaders want we follow fe dem strategy
But fe dem hurry-come-up solution is just another catastrophe
Ah bwoy, modern day slavery
Me seh dem swear dem know whey dem a chat bout
But dem nah talk our language when yu hear from de shout
'Ca as we lift we voice, here comes de perfect plan
Uh Hmm! Nother one fe antagonize we
Nuh de perfect plan
'Cause everyday something increase

Fe mek de likkle money in a we pocket decrease
Tax increase, food price increase, bus fare increase,
        utility rate increase
Yet government tackling poverty
Everyday is a different story
So as de new policy dem frustrate we
We wake up to de reality dat we living in a modern day
        slavery
Fe real dis a modern day slavery
And me nah tek back dat!

Gye Nyame

This world is turning into a battlefield
And so we going out there with our shields
'Ca we not afraid until death we'll fight
'Cause every new day brings a new life
And if a thousand rise up to attack
I have nothing to fear
'Cause this is what I say
Gye Nyame
I fear no one except JAH
Gye Nyame
I fear no one except JAH

So we all trodding upon this battlefield
And to conquer the wicked is our zeal
'Cause their aim is to control the earth
So we going fight for all that it's worth
So even if dem come ten feet tall

Dem going stumble and fall
Again I say Gye Nyame
I fear no one except JAH
Gye Nyame
I fear no one except JAH

Well the just and the unjust still a strifle
But we so confident we heart not troubled
We know who in the end going fall
We know who going stand tall
So be full of courage
The wicked can't flourish
And join me and say Gye Nyame
I fear no one except JAH
Gye Nyame
I fear no one except JAH

Gye Nyame is Ashanti for "I fear no one but my Creator"

ahdri zhina mandiela

dubb aatist, ahdri zhina mandiela has been working on Toronto's theatre scene since the late 70's: from Black Theatre Canada to Young People's Theatre to Nightwood, mandiela has concentrated on developing black women's work for stage.

This quest has taken her through all kinds of creative jaunts with artists old and young/new/not so new/established/ emerging. Text and movement-based material, traditional and contemporary scripts, dramas/comedies, performance/technical/creative /production elements...the works.

Her artist repertoire includes plays, poetry books, audio releases & videos. She's presently artistic director of **b current arts corp,** and looks forward to enhanced development by focusing attention on the aesthetics in black women's performance work.

Photograph by: Michael Chambers

brown sun [i dance a wheel]

ever/y/time/i see/me dance
i dance/where i dance/i dance
a speak/my feet/sound/ing/top my
dancing feet: sing in/to my heart

and then some-
times/i must find/my own way
open my own day/ignite my/brown
sun/dance my own sun/round my
dancing/spinning parts

and when i/dance
my rhythm toes/feel like
dance/spinning toes
beneath my tongue & teeth/singing
flows/beneath my dancing wheel
feels like brown/sun/singing
streams/on my brown sun/spinning
wheels

and then some-
times/i must find my own/way/
then/i may/splay/my rhythm/toes
ignite my frozen woes/let
my heart go/where? it goes

and yes some-
times/i must find/my own/way
my/own/ brown sun/play/my own

[slap/slap/hands/slap]
hands & feet play/hide
& find my own/brown
sun/my own/brown fun
[slap hands/slap hands]
make my own/brown sun
wake my own brown/find my own/brown
/feel my own/brown/i can/feel brown/
i can feel/my own brown/sun/feel my own
i can/brown/sun/makes me feel
/i can/brown sun
makes me feel/i can dance

from/here/to the end/of my brown sun
[i dance a wheel]

my hills are joyful

my hills are joy–
ful in the clouds
murmuring hymns/tuned
to organic strings
in a distant metropolis

rivers from their tops
trickle
thru pipes: cool death
shower cockroaches
clutching at greasy crumbs

in chipped–
enamel sinks. below here
(my hills are joyful)
ancient Arawak skulls
grin constantly
at incensed jokes, gurgled
(and digested)
in powdered marl
(perfumed with kerosene)
and burnt sensimilia herbs
on this eve
of celebrated ritual

and my hills are joy–
ful
in the clouds: where
night/falls/loud/speakers
shriek/pealing bells: dubwise
skanking/jumping
out of oval cell windows
mirroring dreams
of ancestral struggle

free!
free! freedom dances!
from the foot–
hills of my mind

i am now: happy
one last time.

forever

first night

with the breaking
of morning
you called me in

to hear the thoughts
i knew yesterday
the thoughts i knew

two days
a year ago
you called me in
to see the many shades of black
on the walls
hardly trying
to hide the lingering midnight glint
of finger trail shadows on our backs
knowing the night
will come
you called me in

to feel the unhurried motion
of fresh flowers
before the moon drone
arrived
before the light forced our eyes
shut
because the night had come

you called me in
to lay with you
knowing the night will come

first morning i knocked
you called me in.

in the cane fields

her mind has
become
my mouth… her
eyes & ears/my
teeth/my tongue
her feet now planted
in the ground
our stories unsung
except
in the canefields

no more messages in letters
home/no more
sleeping on sultry subways
no more chillblain-boned winter days
only sweet rest in the canefields

my/aunt vida: lithe
bird of youth

took off to canada/surfaced
on a river called don, circled
under dundas bridge: docked
on an edge, lived on a ledge
like the pigeons

no news/papers caught the landing
no taxman demanding
a cut of her nearly unpaid/earning
bread, cooking &
cleaning, making beds
morning & evenings
tending kids she couldn't care about

shopped at *zellers*
woolco & *biway*
shipping a barrel home each holiday
time/pass/new season
spring/summer/finding new
reasons to stick around
no matter that it's under–
ground

she was young, willing &
able/learning french
from food labels
polishing well her accent
for special events/a game
show or lottery winnings:
really only a dream,
in the beginning

& the frayed hopes end
caught her with the same
dream/spent/her bags stamped–
sent home by air/
presents
wrapped in gauze.

unpacked her luggage
in the canefields
buried her baggage
in the canefields: fell
dead/sugar/they said
filled the blood in her head

her mind
has become
my mouth/her
hands & foot & teeth
& tongue/
her tendrils
clinging under–
ground
our story now sung
in the canefields

Mih Feel It
(Wailin fih Mikey)

Dih dred ded
an it dun suh?
No sah

dih dred ded
an it dun suh?

> Ow can a man
> kill annadah one
> wid stone
> cold–
> bludded intenshan
>
> rockstone
> bludgeon im ead
> an
> im drop dung ded
> an nuh one
> nuh awsk
> why
> such a wikkid
> wikkid tawsk
> should
> anna–
> nyah–
> late
> dih dred

Dih dred ded
an it dun suh?
No sah

dih dred ded
an it dun suh?

Early early
inna dih day
Mikey ah trod
dung a illy way

isite up sum men
from a pawty fence
an hence–
forth
was stopped!
wid all dih
chattin weh gwaan
an questions ensued
Mikey painin run out
ah im mout
too soon!
an is den dih trouble
run out

for BAM!
four stone inna dem ans
an BAM!
dem lik Mikey dung

an
mih feel it
mih feel it
mih feel it

Dih dred ded
an it dun suh?
No sah

dih dred ded
an it dun suh?

   ones must know
   dih reason
   for dis deadly
   assault
   committed
   out of season
   no reason
   dred dred dred dred
   season

'Riddemshan for every dred
mus cum
riddemshan
mus cum'

   is dih livity
   not dih rigidity
   for even doah seh

Mikey ded
cause dem mash up
im ead
even doah seh
Mikey gawn
im spirit trod awn
trod awn
tru: RIDDEMSHAN

'Riddemshan for every dred
mus cum
riddemshan
mus cum'

dih dred ded
an it dun suh?

NO SAH!

Cherry Natural

Cherry Natural was born Marcia Wedderburn on April 20, 1960 in Kingston, Jamaica. She attended Kingston Secondary School where she first performed her poetry. Cherry was very inspired at an early age by the work of the legendary Miss Lou, Jamaica's leading folklorist. Cherry recalls, "I admired the way she used the Jamaican language. Her dramatic presentation had a way of bringing out a lot of the social problems during those times".

At the age of sixteen, Cherry enrolled in the Jamaica School of Art, studying graphic and fine arts. Cherry started performing her poetry a cappella in 1979. The tonalities of her voice as well as her consciousness raising lyrics entranced many a listener. The response to her readings encouraged Cherry to enter the Jamaica Cultural Development Commission (JCDC) Pop and Variety Talent Show in 1980. In 1981 Cherry won the talent show, which exposed her on a national level, fostering her confidence and creating future opportunities to perform.

By 1989, Cherry had published her first book, *Come Mek We Reason* and had started performing with her daughter, known as Little Natural. Later that year, she was invited to perform at the annual Woman Trade Fair. She has performed in many major events since then, and released several 'singles' in Jamaica.

Cherry practises several martial arts, namely Tae Kwan Do, Karate, Wing-Chung, Kung Fu and Modern Arnis. She has a Black Belt in Modern Arnis. Cherry believes in balance existing within the mind, soul and body.

Photograph by: Kay Westhues

Youths

Youths unu growing nice
Yes unu growing cute
But if unu no mine weh unu a do
Unu we tun coute
Go to school get some education
Read all the books yu can
Tink big have ambition
Strive to be respectable man an woman
Put what yu learn into practice
Always stan up fe equal rights and justice
Don't get carried away
Mine how unu mix
Or unu we get unu business fix
An we caan afford anymore of this

This Woman

I'm not going to spend my time promoting sex
Cause commercials have already blown it out of context
I am a woman who is political
And I am a woman who is spiritual
I know what I want
I know what I need
I don't believe in greed
Life is very sacred
Anything I'm doing I am committed
Only I can control my emotions

Don't take me simple
I can be as calm as a lamb
And rough as any she lion
I will defend what I believe in to the very end
I have no fears and I naa pretend
I can wage any revolution pon de battle field
And ina yu heart
My passion is so strong, it can be moulded
Into a piece of art
To be exhibited for generations to generations
This woman can melt every bone in your body
And make you shiver with ecstasy
When we get there
I shed tears when I'm coming
Cause I'm so loving
I created beauty with my scenery
Just for the eyes to see
And then I know I have the ability
To turn passion upside down
And blast up a whole town
Cause this woman hates injustice
Capitalistic prejudice
That breeds racism and sexism
This woman is wild
This woman is natural
Cannot be coaxed when the adrenaline flows
Save your energy, it's easier to join
Than to change me
This woman is on the loose.

Come Mek We Reason

Come jam sit een an reason wid me
Come mek we reason bout love
Come mek we reason bout peace
Come mek we reason pon reality
Hold a spot feel irie
Block di negatives from yu mind
Come hurry up we nuh have much time
Come mek we reason
A long time we fi reason
Yes we fe reason
In an out a season

I woulda like fe know if all wha a gwaan
Use to gwaan before I an I born
An a wanda if a so dem inten fe carry aan
Did you know dat our system is leaking
Yes de system needs fixing
An I'm not jokin
Stick a pin
What woulda happen
If we nevah have Garvey
Nanny
Bob Marley
Een, tell me
Yu tink it easy to be black
An livin in pavety, weh yu sey? Man go
Hole yu gravity
Cause you tink it easy to be surrounded by immorality
Hypocrisy and loss of dignity

What we gonna do to save humanity
Tell me, tell me
Instead of fighting each other
Why not come een, sit een an reason bout de matta
Yu have sarrow, well go tell it to de breeze
Or de trees, if you don't want to reason
A sure know dem not goin hear, and even
If they did they sure wouldn't care

So yu se why people fe reason
Yes we fe reason
We haffi reason
In an out a season
Wuk pon a plan
To get a solution
An break dung de corruption

I'm Walking Out Of Your Jail Tonight
For Emancipation Day

Take a good look at me
Make a mental picture
capture all the details
Put them on your computer
I'm walking out of your jail tonight
Yes I'm walking out of your jail tonight
I'm gonna break those bars and set myself free
hire all the security that you can

Give them your weapon of destruction
that won't stop me
I'm walking out of your jail tonight
Yes I'm walking out of your jail tonight
You have had your time and that's enough
I'm giving you back your man made rules
I'm giving you back your colonial attitudes
Take your laws out of my life
Your standards are not mine
If it is the last thing I be
I'm gonna be me
This spirit of mine must be free
so I'm walking out of your jail tonight
Yes I'm walking out of your jail tonight
I'm leaving the things you used to
control my mind, behind
You feed me with your hate, your jealousy,
Your greed, your guns and your drugs
Making me into the people's enemy
I say no more, I will take no more
I'm walking out of your jail tonight
Yes I'm walking out of your jail tonight
No amount of money can stop me
True wealth goes beyond possession
Call me insane, this time I won't complain
Madness has a way of freeing the soul
One more black woman is gonna be free
I'm walking out of your jail tonight, tonight, tonight

Feel De Pressure

Hey unu feel it
Unu no feel it?
Me sey unu no feel how de pressure jus a circulate
Tru me structure
Unu no feel de cry of a baby madda
Who get pregnant an don know de fadda
Feel de pressure nuh
Feel de pressure of a youth weh wake up in de morning
An all him have fe breakfast
Is two bad wod flying from de mout of him madda
Feel de pressure an no badda complain
Feel de pressure an no badda mek no blame
Because she cyaan do no betta
De poor woman unda pressure
A so she know it, an a so she show it
Feel de pressure of a young man jus leave school
an lookin for wuk
Him walk from agency to agency
All him hear a pure nancy story
Come back home wid vengance in him heart
Sidung, an give up knowing that is not his fault
Feel de pressure an no badda complain
Feel de pressure an ask who is to blame
At de same time de big man dem siddung
ina dem concrete castle
Lean back ina dem easy chair widout a care
Heart at ease, mind well contented
Meanwhile dung ina de ghetto
White squale a bide, house a leak, cupboard empty,

cockroach an fly plenty
So feel de pressure nuh, feel de pressure!
Feel de pressure an reach out an give a helping han
Because we all human.

Gold Chain Mentality

Cho
Gold chain mentality
Gold chain mentality
It na go hold me
No it caan hold me
An no mek it hold yu
Me a beg yu do
It we mek yu do tings
Yu don't want fe do
Like stealing an selling yu body
To have a good name
Seeking fame
With a couple gold chain
Is a worthless game
Jewels from yu neck
Straight dung to yu toe
Mek yu faba pappyshow
Nuff a who yu see have aan a whole heap a jewellery
If yu check it out dem a dead fe hungry
An every minute dem sick cause dem nuh healthy
De money weh dem fi tek pay doctor bill
Dem prefa tek it pay dung pon jewel

Deanne Smith a.k.a Dee

Deanne Smith a.k.a. Dee is a poet and spoken word artist, who has been writing and performing for the past eight years. She recently relocated to Toronto from Montreal where she lived for twelve years.

Dee's writing reflect socio-political and women's issues, personal experiences and a bit of "everyday living" dramas. She is very opinionated in her written and oral expressions, but takes time to reflect before doing so. In addition to making time to attend cultural dance and musical performances, she finds herself quite passionate about playing the *Djembe* (an African traditional drum) and the guitar, both of which she hopes to master at some point in her life.

Dee is an easy-going, fun loving individual and likes travelling and learning about other cultures and languages. She is presently studying Engineering Technology and hopes to be an innovative Engineer whose creation is relevant in fostering a more enriched human experience.

Shit - U - A - Shun

What a hell What a hell
what a shit-u-a-shun
hard life a tek di poor a di nation
What a hell What a hell
what a con-di-tion
some willing fi sell dem reputation

Fi promotion & prestige
some willing fi seize
care not if dem use
underhanded means
minorities dispossess
exposed by di press
collect an amount
if yuh willing to sell out

What a hell What a hell
sticky shit-u-a-shun
no new plans fi alleviation
What a hell What a hell
mental starvation
unwanted few in a critical condition

Di disease call poor
some cant tek it nuh more
dem totally flip out
an a tek a hand out
in a dis yah democratic society
some a live off a charity

money a di priority
an not humanity

What a hell What a hell
trial & tribulation
going about new arbitration
What a hell What a hell
fi change di shit-u-a-shun
we have fi come up wid newer creation

Seeping Things

Banjoman playing
ketch granny Mento dancing
while folk singers recount stories
in melodic voices

Pickney dem ring ding playing
round fire side
where BIG women
roast breadfruit & saltfish

Drumskin echoing/calling
prepare fi duh di "Brukins"
di spirit dem waiting / anticipating
dis "POCO REVIVAL" time...

Bradah 2 Bradah

Bradah 2 Bradah – Bradah 2 Bradah (check)
Bradah 2 Bradah – Bradah 2 Bradah (one's)
Bradah 2 Bradah – Bradah 2 Bradah (time)

Bradah to Bradah uhnu suh unkind
what happen uhnu lass uhnu mind
Bradah to Bradah uhnu out a line
boasting about uhnu gun crime

Bradah to Bradah what is uhnu aim
living a life fi grave yard to gain
Bradah to Bradah uhnu nuh have nuh shame
stop playing mi-sogy-nis-tic games

Bradah to Bradah uhnu a sing bout
gal fi come skin out…
after uhnu madah labour & push uhnu out
Clean up uhnu negative lyrics
Use positive writing tactics

Bradah to Bradah uhnu fi mek haste
educational opportunity must never waste
Bradah to Bradah be a man
pon woman NUH put uhnu hand

Bradah to Bradah now is high time
tek uhnu family out a di welfare line
Bradah to Bradah
together

work more
stop moving from skid row
unto
death row

Bradah 2 Bradah – Bradah 2 Bradah (check)
Bradah 2 Bradah – Bradah 2 Bradah (one's)
Bradah 2 Bradah – Bradah 2 Bradah (time)
WHY !
Uhnu 2 young to die

SCRIBING that I am

I am the writer who
doesn't like to write
with a pen
prefers the head instead

The writer who writes in the sky

I am the writer you see in the streets
writing while walking
writing hard
writing strong
writing long
smiling

The writer who writes in style

I am the writer who
writes outside in / inside out
cryptic words bouncing about

I am the writer who
doesn't like to write
in black & white
cause colour has more valour

The writer who is lighting with writing

Anita Stewart a.k.a Anilia Soyinka

Anita Stewart a.k.a Anilia Soyinka is a community worker, performing artist and poet. She studied theatre-in-education at the Edna Manly School for the Visual and Performing Arts in Jamaica and worked as a Specialist Teacher in the school system while using Popular Theater to educate the wider community. She has performed in North America, Europe and the Caribbean. Her published and recorded work to date include selected pieces in the anthology *Dub Poetry – Nineteen Poets from England and Jamaica* published in Germany by Christian Haberkost, and the all female Dub Poetry album *Woman Talk* which was produced by Mutabaruka in Jamaica. Anilia has a degree in psychology and intends to do further studies after taking a break. She is the proud mother of a very talented daughter, Debbie, whom she believes has given her more than enough reason to continue the struggle which life demands. She does believe that the pen is mightier than the sword and uses it to guide her in her day to day living.

Photograph by: Abida Sherazee

Diasporic Homelessness

evah since i was captured
   and stolen from afrika
      i have no resting place
        i am an afrikan
          wid a nomadic fate
            wherevah i sleep at nights
              dats my home

sometime i bounce it pon di subway
another time it's di overpass pon di highway
nex time a di piazza in di city
or is the sewer pipe dat look alright
of course inside is well well messy
last night it was a little shack
by the cargo train track
tomorrow it gwine to rain
i might have to hed fi di plane
in di millitary park
i caan skylark
no i caan skylark
cause...... evah since I was captured
      and stolen from Afrika
        i ave no resting place
       i am an afrikan wid a nomadic fate
          wherevah i sleep at nights
            dats my home

couple nights well
i taught di farmah rin' di bell
but was calling strictly membas of the rodent family

cause i was cornered back to back
an belly to belly in the ally
by 'undreds of giant-size, middle-size
teeny-weeny, creepy, craawly
knawin', nibblin', flying,
rats, mice, bats whatevah you call dat
which wanted to attak
i had to dive in a tunnel of sh...
sheeeeee...something saaft
and aftah all dat i still had to laff
cause......evah since i was captured
          an stolen from afrika
              i ave no resting place
              i am an afrikan wid a nomadic fate
                    wherevah i sleep at nights
                        dats my home

i rememba one winta
i had couple sheets a newspapah
lots of cardboard
cause i decide to hoard dem from summah
madda always tell me
put away someting for di rainy day
dis time it wasn't wata
it was i—c—e
six a one half dozen a di odda
can yuh imagin mi pitching my caadboard tent
trying fi seal all di vents
to barrikade the brazen cold
attaking a tropical soul
f-r-e-e-z-ing a lost spirit
still i haffi chill

and be grateful fi di will
to sur—vi—ve
stay a—li—ve
cause evah since i was captured
            an stolen from afrika
                i ave no resting place
                      mi is a afrikan
                          wid a nomadic fate
                            enny weh mi sleep a nite time
                                dat is mi 'ome

w'en yuh see mi bouncing here
troddin' dere
trying to get comfatable in a caana
don't badda tun up yu nose and cock yuh yeye glass
now dat...wi meck mi cuss pure rass
i waan to remin' everyone of
di royal blood in dese veins
my foreparent dem a did king and queen who used to reign
and i have a 'ome in the madda lan'
but it was wrenched from mi foreparent dem 'ans
by teif who tek it for dem own now lef i fi roam
yes dem tek it for dem own and lef i fi roam

when you si mi transporting mi bed
a nuh nuh spechal event
mi nuh need no audience
this happen every night
soh jus....keep you snabbish comment to yuhself
nuh call i a vagrant
or try fi make mi feel smaaall
like an ant

this situashan is transishanal
i am of the convikshan that the circle
will be completed
and i will
retrieve
what was depleted
s–e–e–n!!

but...ever since i was captured
          and stolen from africa
               i have no resting place
               i am an african with a nomadic fate
                    where ever i sleep at nights
                         dats my home,

TEMOROARILY
          dats my home
                    TEMPORARILY DAT IS!!!
                         dats my home
          I SAID TEMPORARILY – TEMPORARILY dat is!!!

in the mean time i
keep trodding wid
mi bundle a sorrows an
dat of mi madda
mi dadda
 and mi sister dem.

Beggin is a Ting

chorus:
begging is a ting
a carry di swing
inna dis ya time
it cyaan be a crime
begging is a ting
a carry di swing
inna dis ya time
it cyaan be crime

ah walk down town
one a dem days
had to stan up for a while
and tek a good gaze
di city is plagued an' reach di stage
dat... chorus

madman a beg seh im nuh ave no bread
car man answer "you must be loosing your head
i should take my money give you something to eat
find yourself a job and get off of the street
yes find yourself a job and get off the street."

if i could find miself a job
mi would come off a di street
...chorus

youth deh a stoplight a wipe windscreen
"beg you a ten cent mam si de glass clean"
solution to di problem by de law-claim police

charge di pickney an further force dem fi teif
lock dem inna jail t'row di time
now who give a dam if punishment
 nuh fit di time
…chorus

Riding on a bus hear a woman a cuss
"mi baby faada resent me wid di ten pickney
so mi lass resort nuh fi start?
walking in di city an' beg
hope seh mi get more dan pity

hope sey mi get some clothes pon mi back
an' likkle food inna mi belly"
…chorus

went to di bank today
as a reach di door ah hear somebady say
"PITY THE POOR"
ah see a man wid a pan in im han
di pan was labelled
"HELP THE DIFFERENTLY ABLED"
went to the church hear parson a preach
"give what you have and the
lord will give you more
give what you have for there is
something more in store
give what you have"
as im start emulate christ
wid di collection plate
…chorus

mi tink to miself
when it get cold
does di beggar ever come inna di holy
warmth a di church and worship god
no!
him jus a trod
beggar nuh go church fi di fear a de rod
an di shout......
"Get Out!!"

An still
begging is a ting
a carry di swing
inna dis ya time
it can't be a crime
political war cause people to starve
economik crisis
put di victims on the beggers list
even wid massive homelessness
di politicians still nuh get
dat begging is a ting
a carry di swing
inna dis ya time it cyaan be a crime
sey begging is a ting a carry di swing
inna dis ya time how it fi be a crime.

Spice Island Slaughter
(Tribute to all those who perished in the
Grenadian invasion)

the troop dem come like
thief inna di night
and blood drip
di fascist tek a sip
blood drip
an di fascist tek sip

yes a sip a di wine
fermented in di malnourished
baadys of the proletariats
fi dem blood get shed
the scene get red
spice isle
people start bawl
mutilated dem fall
helpless
dispossessed

while......blood drip – drip – drip
the big man tek a sip
blood drip – drip – drip
an still di troops keep
komming... komming
komming sout'
komming from up north
dem sey...
fi get rid a di commies

eliminate di risk
eliminate di root
a di working class movement
an di troops keep komming

sufferers try fi scattah
but bones staat shattah
marrow staat fi fly and
innocent people die…die…die
killed……and blood drip
drip — drip
and the fascist tek a sip
yes blood a drip
blood a run and di fascist
still a sip
yes blood a run

sip a-a-a-n mr. big fella
yuh a go sip yuh way
to the tap a di slaughter ladda
den to tek a d — i — v — e
try to ser-v-i-ve nuh
but it a go too late
di ladda will be fake
den time
fi yoo-oor bloody fall
wid yuh back against di wall
what yuh see in front yuh yeye
look
nuh badda cry
nuh badda cry
blood vision…

blood-bath people...
suffering
why??????
lives slipping by
beneath dere feet
blood stone
blood earth
blood seed
blood weed
bloody hair
blood-torn clothes
blood-flowing tears
heart beat bloody beats
ears hear bleeding s-c-r-e-a-m-s
head squirt plasma
and asses flame
red-----hot-----hurt

pure raw
raw blood
it still a drip
do you insist to sip
of the bishop's blood
where was di priest to
consecrate di mass grave
of innocence
di revolushan will not be forgotten
morris..cannat be erased...morris...will not be forgotten!!!

Level Vibes

chorus:
long long time
wi nuh ave nuh nice time
come mek wi ave a likkle nice time nuh
mi sey a long long time
wi nuh ave nuh nice time
come mek we ave a likkle nice time nuh

come mek we nack heads
sip some juice
cook ital stew
play dominoes
'cause... chorus

mek we sip some wine
eat some cheese
it nuh spell sense
if wi try to be mean
share some smiles
even for a while
cause... chorus

how about playing some music
any kind a music
could be jazz, r & b
classical, country,
i mean any kind a music
of course fi me
is reggae music
di likkle weh we ave

we haffi utilize it
turn up di soun system
although wi conscious
a di isims and skisims weh a gwaan
mek we jump and prance
inna dis ya dance
fi ave some fun
cause some fun nuh laas long
an di fun nuh soon done????
and... chorus

mek we
push som drums in high gear
so di drum beat
is di heart beat yuh hear
drums talking
di rhythms barking
nuff drum a talk
and di rhythms a bark
it is the voice of our souls
sounding, echoing
people loving , sharing, caring, enjoying
cause... chorus

and when you feel di feel
dat i want yu to feel
then move it
come an feel di feel
dat i want yu to feel
and rock it
i sey to rock it

when you feel it
nuh try fi squeeze it
jus' reveal it
don' be afraid
to gyrate and gwaan bad
i mean get in the mood
move to the groove
and let the good vibe flow
level vibes flow
because a long long time
wi nuh ave no nice time
come mek we ave a likkle nice time nuh
mek we ave a likkle nice time
ave a likkle nice time
ave a likkle nice time now!

Select Bibliography

BOOKS

COOPER, CAROLYN, *Noises in the Blood: Orality, Gender and the "Vulgar" Body in Jamaican Popular Culture* (Durham: Duke University Press, 1995).

DAWES, KWAME, ed. *Wheel and Come Again: An Anthology of Reggae Poetry* (Fredericton, New Brunswick: Goose Lane, 1998).

ESPINET, RAMABAI , ed. *Creation Fire, A CAFRA Anthology of Caribbean Women's Poetry* (Toronto: Sister Vision Press, 1990).

HABEKOST, CHRISTIAN, *Verbal Riddims, The Politics and Aesthetics of African-Caribbean Dub Poetry* (Amsterdam: Rodopi, 1993).

HURSTON, ZORA NEALE , *Tell My Horse* (Philadelphia: J.B. Lippincott, 1938).

MORDECAI, PAMELA & MORRIS, MERVYN; eds. *Jamaica Woman: An Anthology of Poems* (Kingston, Jamaica: Heineman, 1980).

MURRELL, NATHANIEL SAMUEL, ed. *Chanting Down Babylon: The Rastafari Reader* (Temple University Press, 1998).

POLLARD, VELMA, *Dread Talk: The Language of Rastafari* (Kingston, Jamaica: Canoe Press, 1994).

TANA, LAURA, *Jamaican Folk Tales and Oral Histories* (Kingston, Jamaica: Institute of Jamaica, 1984).

ARTICLES AND PAPERS

COOPER, AFUA, "African Oral Tradition and Caribbean Dub Poetry: The Canadian Case," Paper presented at African Roots of Caribbean Culture, Florida A & M University, Tallahassee, Florida, April 1995.

"Rhythm and Resistance, Maintaining the Social Connection," *Fuse Magazine* interview with 'de dub poets,' Lillian Allen, Devon Haughton, and Clifton Joseph, Toronto, Summer 1983.

The editor and the publisher would like to thank the following for their kind permission to reprint copyright material in this book.

Lillian Allen: 'Tribute to Miss Lou', *Women Do This Everyday* (Toronto: Women's Press, 1993), 'Riddim An' Hardtimes', *Riddim An' Hardtimes* (Toronto: Domestic Bliss, 1982). Louise Bennett: 'Bans O' Ooman', 'Dutty Tough', *Jamaica Labrish* (Kingston, Jamaica: Sangsters, 1966); 'Bans A Killin', *Selected Poems* (Kingston, Jamaica: Sangsters, 1982). Jean 'Binta' Breeze: 'Dubwise', 'Warner', *Riddym Ravings* (London: Race Today, 1988); 'Homecoming (One)', 'Mermaids', *Spring Cleaning* (London: Virago Press, 1992); 'Grandfather's Dreams', 'Pipe Woman', *On The Edge of An Island* (London: Bloodaxe). Michelle Barrow: 'Rebellious Red', Kendel Hippolyte, ed. *So Much Poetry In We People*. Afua Cooper: 'Memories Have Tongue', 'A True Revolution', *Memories Have Tongue* (Toronto: Sister Vision Press, 1992); 'Birds of Paradise', 'At The Centre', 'Woman A Wail', *Understatement*, Tanya Nanavati, ed. (Toronto: Seraphim Editions, 1996). ahdri ahina mandiela: 'Mih Feel It—Wailin Fih Mikey', *Speshal Rikwes* (Toronto: Sister Vision Press, 1985); 'In The Canefields', *dark diaspora in dub* (Toronto: Sister Vision Press, 1991). Cherry Natural: 'Come Meck We Reason', 'Feel De Pressure', 'Gold Chain Mentality', *Come Meck We Reason* (Kingston, Jamaica: Careso, 1989). Anita Stewart a.k.a Anilia Soyinka: 'Beggin is a Ting', *Woman Talk* (Kingston, Jamaica: Mutabaruka, 1984)